Meet the HOUSTON TEXANS

By
ZACK BURGESS

BIG PICTURE Sports

Norwood House Press
CHICAGO, ILLINOIS

Norwood House Press

P.O. Box 316598 • Chicago, Illinois 60631
For more information about Norwood House Press please visit our website at www.norwoodhousepress.com or call 866-565-2900.

Photo Credits:

All photos courtesy of Associated Press, except for the following: Topps, Inc. (6, 10 both, 11 all), Black Book Archives (7, 18, 23).

Cover Photo: G. Newman Lowrance/Associated Press

The football memorabilia photographed for this book is part of the authors' collection. The collectibles used for artistic background purposes in this series were manufactured by many different card companies—including Bowman, Donruss, Fleer, Leaf, O-Pee-Chee, Pacific, Panini America, Philadelphia Chewing Gum, Pinnacle, Pro Line, Pro Set, Score, Topps, and Upper Deck—as well as several food brands, including Crane's, Hostess, Kellogg's, McDonald's and Post.

Designer: Ron Jaffe
Series Editors: Mike Kennedy and Mark Stewart
Project Management: Black Book Partners, LLC.
Editorial Production: Lisa Walsh

LIBRARY OF CONGRESS CATALOGING-IN-PUBLICATION DATA

Names: Burgess, Zack.
Title: Meet the Houston Texans / by Zack Burgess.
Description: Chicago, Illinois : Norwood House Press, 2016. | Series: Big picture sports | Includes bibliographical references and index. | Audience: Grade: K to Grade 3.
Identifiers: LCCN 2015026330| ISBN 9781599537504 (Library Edition : alk. paper) | ISBN 9781603578530 (eBook)
Subjects: LCSH: Houston Texans (Football team)--Miscellanea--Juvenile literature.
Classification: LCC GV956.H69 B87 2016 | DDC 796.332/64097642812--dc23
LC record available at http://lccn.loc.gov/2015026330

© 2017 by Norwood House Press. All rights reserved.
No part of this book may be reproduced without written permission from the publisher.
The Houston Texans is a registered trademark of Houston NFL Holdings, L.P.
This publication is not affiliated with the Houston Texans, Houston NFL Holdings, L.P.,
The National Football League, or The National Football League Players Association.

288N–072016
Manufactured in the United States of America in North Mankato, Minnesota

CONTENTS

Call Me a Texan 5
Time Machine 6
Best Seat in the House 9
Shoe Box 10
The Big Picture 12
True or False? 14
Go Texans, Go! 17
On the Map 18
Home and Away 20
We Won! 22
Record Book 23
Football Words 24
Index 24
About the Author 24

Words in **bold type** are defined on page 24.

The Texans celebrate a touchdown.

CALL ME A TEXAN

"Don't mess with Texas." This has been a popular saying for a long time. Teams in the National Football League (NFL) don't like messing with the Houston Texans. They tackle hard and are quick on their feet. The Texans are fun to watch but not to play!

TIME MACHINE

The Texans played their first season in the National Football League (NFL) in 2002. They were not the first football team in Houston. From 1960 to 1996, a team called the Oilers played there. The Texans built their team around a great defense led by **J.J. Watt**. Andre Johnson was the team's biggest star on offense.

Andre Johnson caught the most passes in team history.

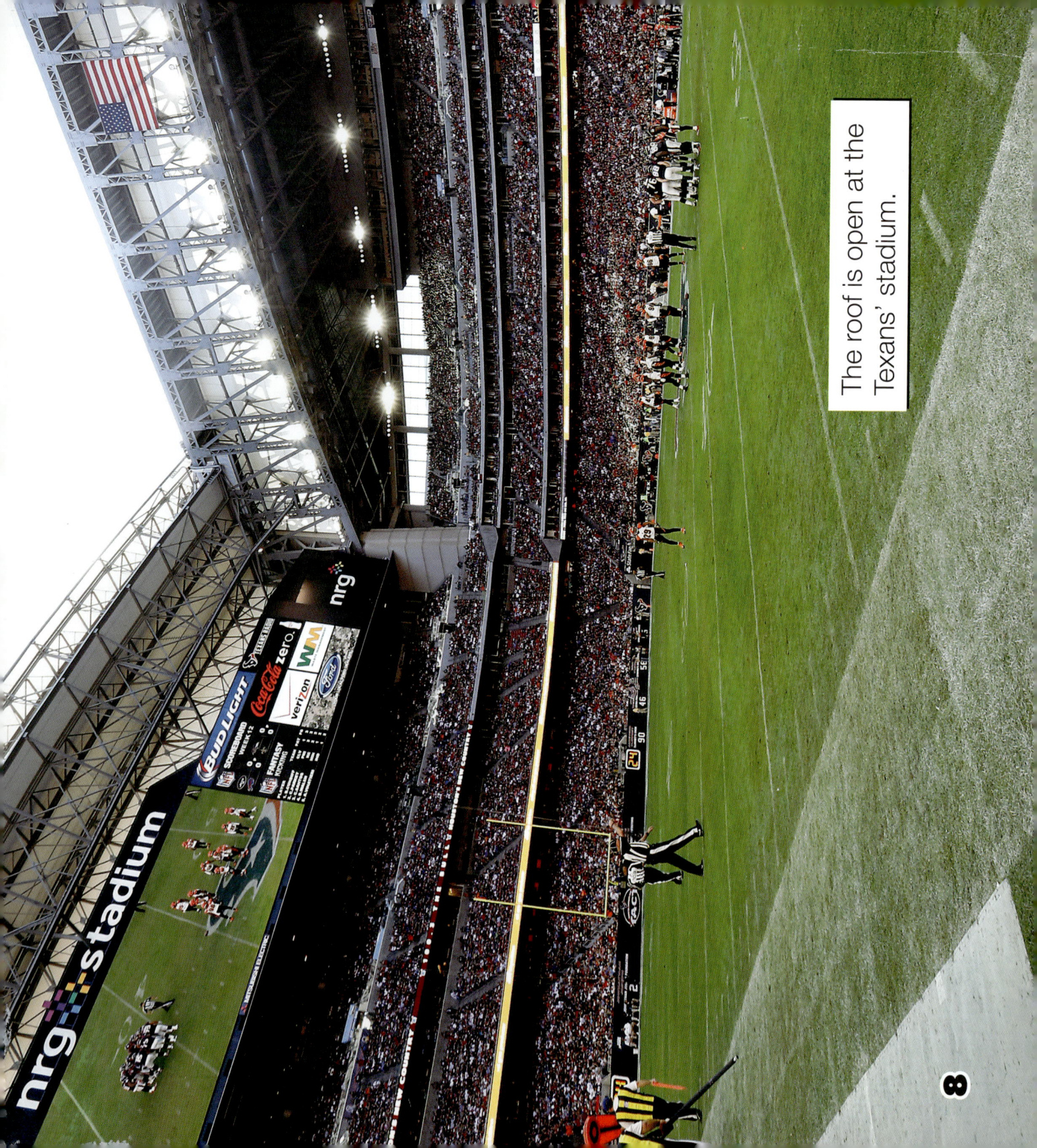

The roof is open at the Texans' stadium.

BEST SEAT IN THE HOUSE

The Texans' stadium has a roof that opens and closes in just seven minutes. That means fans are protected even if there is a sudden storm. The stadium also hosts rodeos and concerts. More than two million people attend events there every year.

Shoe Box

The trading cards on these pages show some of the best Texans ever.

Andre Johnson
Receiver · 2003–2014
Andre was big, fast, and had great hands. He caught more than 100 passes in five seasons.

DeMeco Ryans
Linebacker · 2006–2011
DeMeco was a star in his first season with Houston. He played in the **Pro Bowl** twice as a Texan.

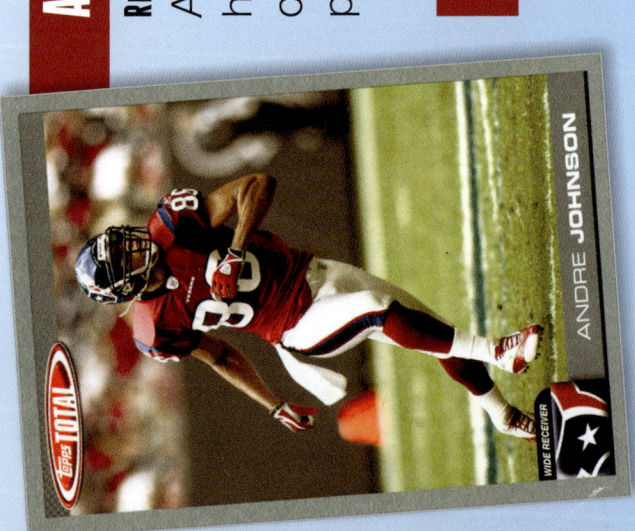

MATT SCHAUB

QUARTERBACK · 2007–2013

The Texans became a winning team after they traded for Matt. In 2009, he was the NFL's top passer.

DUANE BROWN

TACKLE · FIRST YEAR WITH TEAM: 2008

Few linemen were better than Duane at protecting the quarterback. He was an **All-Pro** in 2012.

ARIAN FOSTER

RUNNING BACK · FIRST YEAR WITH TEAM: 2009

Arian was a threat as a runner and a receiver. In 2010 and then again in 2015, he led the NFL in rushing touchdowns.

The Big Picture

Look at the two photos on page 13. Both appear to be the same. But they are not. There are three differences. Can you spot them?

Answers on page 23.

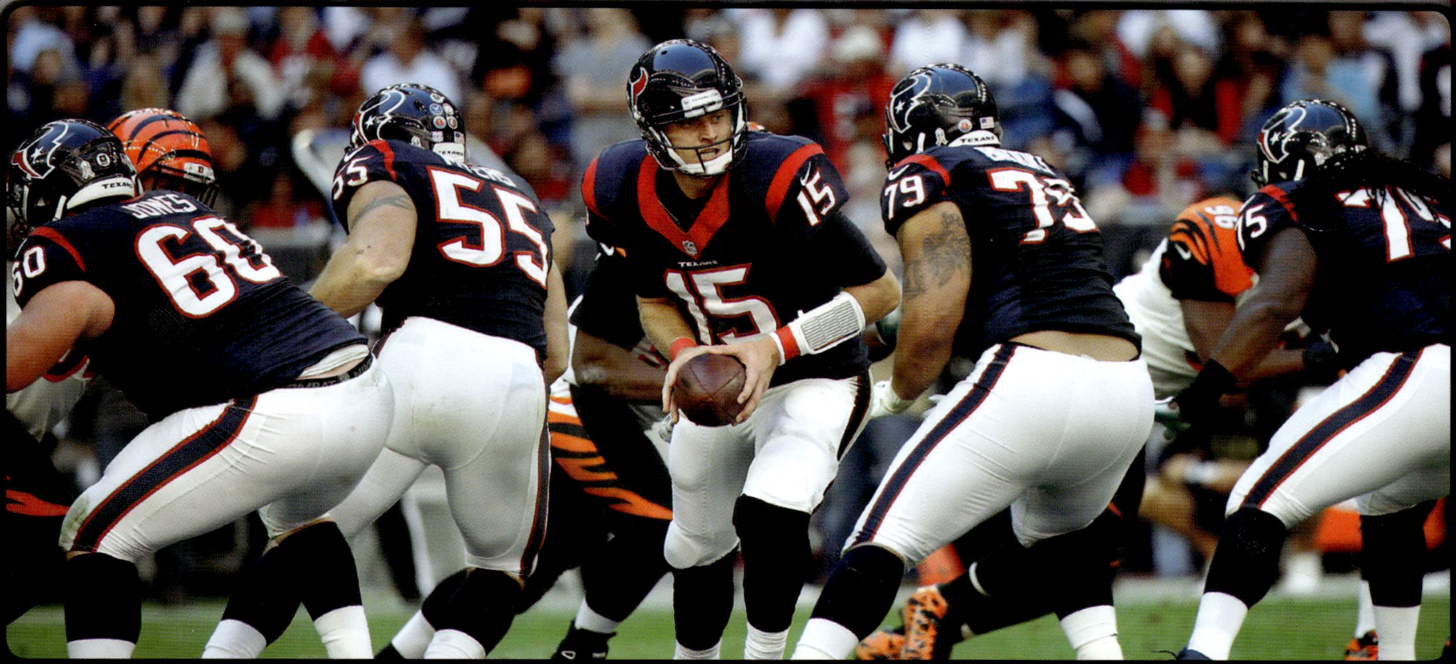

JONES
60
55
15
79
75

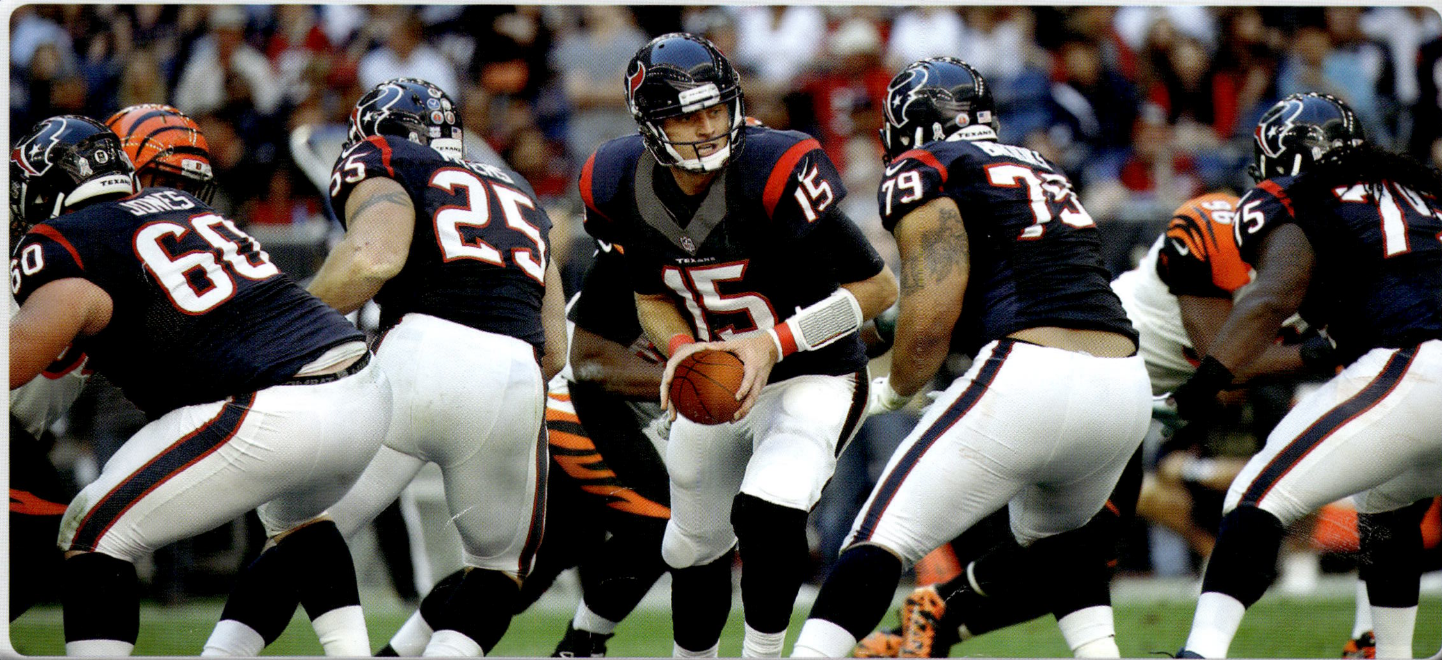

JONES
60
25
15
79
75

TRUE OR FALSE?

J.J. Watt was a star defender. Two of these facts about him are **TRUE**. One is **FALSE**. Do you know which is which?

1. J.J. was the NFL Defensive Player of the Year in 2012, 2014, and 2015.

2. J.J.'s teammates called him the "99 Watt Bulb."

3. J.J. was the first NFL player with at least 20 **quarterback sacks** in two different seasons.

Answer on page 23.

No player was more exciting to watch than J.J. Watt.

The Texans celebrate a score on Battle Red Day.

GO TEXANS, GO!

A few times every year, the Texans celebrate Battle Red Day. It is a fun way to support the team. The players wear bright red uniforms. The fans, cheerleaders, and the Bull Pen Band also dress in red. Even Toro the Bull wears red.

On the Map

Here is a look at where five Texans were born, along with a fun fact about each.

1. **OWEN DANIELS · NAPERVILLE, ILLINOIS**
Owen caught 385 passes for the Texans.

2. **BRIAN CUSHING · PARK RIDGE, NEW JERSEY**
Brian had 134 tackles in his first year as a Texan.

3. **MARIO WILLIAMS · RICHLANDS, NORTH CAROLINA**
Mario played in the Pro Bowl twice for the Texans.

4. **CHRIS MYERS · MIAMI, FLORIDA**
Chris made the Pro Bowl in 2011 and 2012.

5. **AMOBI OKOYE · ANAMBRA, NIGERIA**
As a 20-year-old, Amobi had 5.5 quarterback sacks for the Texans.

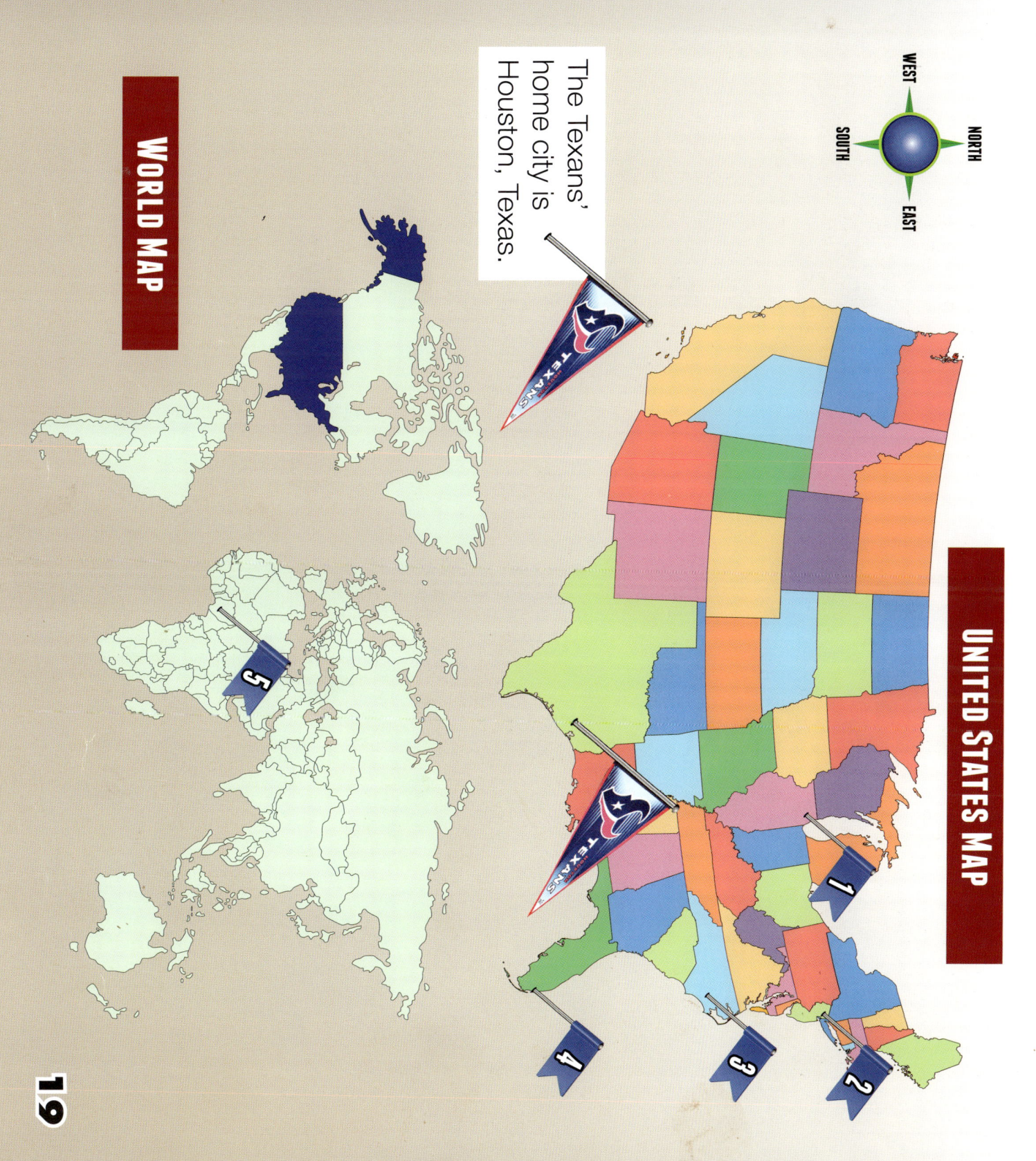

HOME AND AWAY

Football teams wear different uniforms for home and away games. The main colors of the Texans are red, white, and dark blue. These are also the colors of the Texas flag.

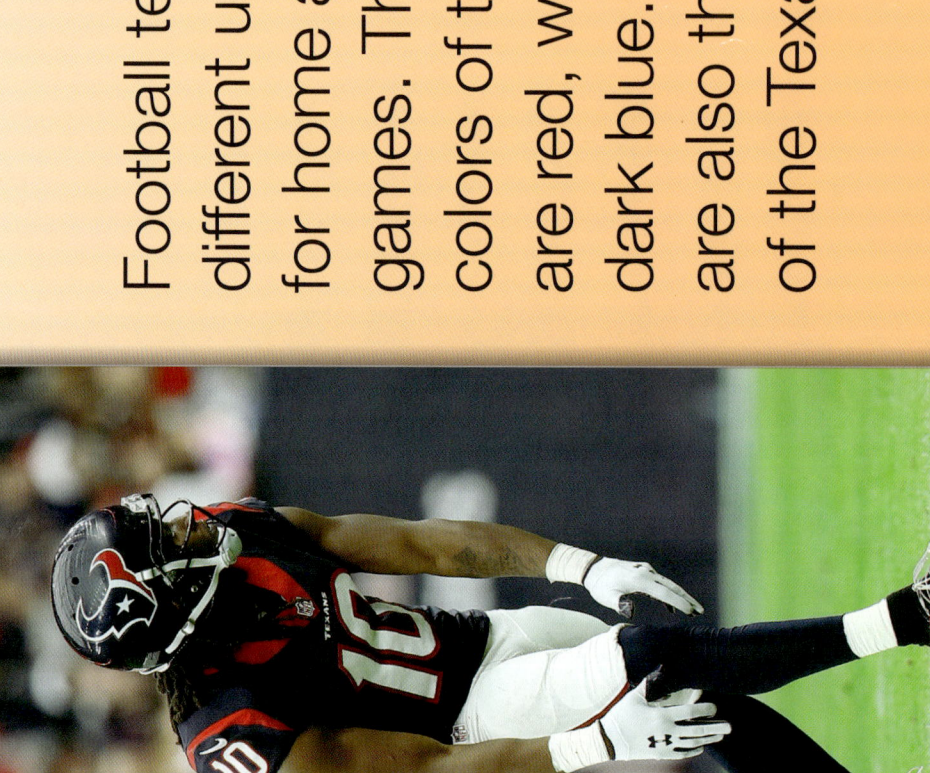

DeAndre Hopkins wears the Texans' home uniform.

The Texans' helmet is blue. There is a bull's head on each side. The bull's eye is the famous lone star of Texas.

Johnathan Joseph wears the Texans' away uniform.

WE WON!

The Texans had their first winning season in 2009. In 2011, they made the **playoffs** for the first time. One player who helped turn things around was **J.J. Watt**. He made the Houston defense one of the NFL's best.

RECORD BOOK

These Texans set team records.

Touchdown Passes

	RECORD
Season: Matt Schaub (2009)	29
Career: Matt Schaub	124

Touchdown Catches

	RECORD
Season: DeAndre Hopkins (2015)	11
Career: **Andre Johnson**	64

Rushing Touchdowns

	RECORD
Season: Arian Foster (2010)	16
Career: Arian Foster	54

Answers for The Big Picture
#55 changed to #25, the stripe on the collar of #15's jersey changed to gray, and the football changed to a basketball.

Answer for True and False
#2 is false. J.J. was not called the "99 Watt Bulb."

Index

Brown, Duane	11, **11**
Cushing, Brian	18, **18**
Daniels, Owen	18
Foster, Arian	11, **11**, 23
Hopkins, DeAndre	**20**, 23
Johnson, Andre	6, 7, 10, **10**, 23, **23**
Joseph, Johnathan	**21**
Myers, Chris	18
Okoye, Amobi	18
Ryans, DeMeco	10, **10**
Schaub, Matt	11, **11**, 23
Watt, J.J.	6, **6**, 14, **15**, 22, **22**
Williams, Mario	18

Photos are on **BOLD** numbered pages.

Football Words

All-Pro
An honor given to the best NFL player at each position.

Playoffs
The games played after the regular season that decide which teams will play in the Super Bowl.

Pro Bowl
The NFL's annual all-star game.

Quarterback Sacks
Tackles of the quarterback that lose yardage.

About the Author

Zack Burgess has been writing about sports for more than 20 years. He has lived all over the country and interviewed lots of All-Pro football players, including Brett Favre, Eddie George, Jerome Bettis, Shannon Sharpe, and Rich Gannon. Zack was the first African American beat writer to cover Major League Baseball when he worked for the *Kansas City Star*.

About the Texans

Learn more at these websites:

www.houstontexans.com • www.profootballhof.com
www.teamspiritextras.com/Overtime/html/texans.html